Ask Master Mom

MOM

Masterful Parenting with Master Mom®

by

Amanda Olson

Disclaimer

The information contained in this eBook is offered for informational purposes solely, and it is geared towards providing exact and reliable information in regards to the topic and issue covered. The author and the publisher does not warrant that the information contained in this e-book is fully complete and shall not be responsible for any errors or omissions.

The author and publisher shall have neither liability nor responsibility to any person or entity concerning any reparation, damages, or monetary loss caused or alleged to be caused directly or indirectly by this e-book. Therefore, this eBook should be used as a guide - not as the ultimate source.

The publication is sold with the idea that the publisher is not required to render accounting, officially permitted, or otherwise, qualified services. If advice is necessary, legal or professional, a practiced individual in the profession should be ordered.

Table of Contents

From The Author...

My name is Amanda Olson and I have two kids of my own, both grown. And, as of this writing both are engaged to be married this year. (I am secretly hoping in a few years to write about Masterful Grandparenting!)

Some of you may be saying, "Only two kids?" That's it? How hard could it be? I understand your skepticism; however, I have 1,000's of martial arts children who I have helped raise. Children I have raised from very young to now having children of their own, living their lives and hopefully passing on the lessons I so carefully and sometimes a little compellingly taught them.

After working with 1000's of families over the past 35 years in so many different capacities I may have not seen every problem (and success) but it's pretty close. I am a true believer in "It takes a village to raise a child" so think of me as part of your village. An empathetic, experienced ear, and a source of wisdom while you navigate these early through teen years of parenting. There is very little I haven't seen or experienced firsthand, either through raising my own children, or helping other families navigate the tricky waters of parenting through the years.

My training in child rearing began with my little brother. Not that my parents weren't doing a great job, but I was the big sister and for whatever reason took it upon myself to take on the task of teaching him everything I knew about life. From when to be quiet, to how to make it look like you ate most of your peas and carrots off the plate at dinner. I am happy to say he has grown up to be a well-adjusted member of society with five children of his own despite my unsolicited mothering.

In all seriousness though, I am a Master Martial Artist in Taekwondo and a Master Instructor. In my martial arts association, it takes about three years to earn a black belt. It then takes two more years to earn a 2nd degree black belt, 2 years to earn a 3rd degree, 3 years to earn a 4th degree and on and on adding an extra year for each rank. I earned my Master Instructor Rank in 2002 and earned my most recent rank of 8th degree black belt in 2014. I am aspiring to the rank of 9th degree black belt which I will be eligible for in the way-off-sounding year of 2022. I have not taken a break during this time in my career. I continue to teach classes for students of all levels. I teach instructors how to teach and how to communicate effectively with students of all ages. I have worked with children with every imaginable issue. Children with ADD, ADHD, Downs syndrome, physical disabilities, hearing impaired, rebellious, autism at many levels, abused – physically & mentally, OCD and ODD, children who have been bullied, children who are bullies, timid children, strongwilled children, the class clown and really, in the last three and a half decades... everything!

I have helped children go from unfocused little devils to respectful and happy members of the community. I have helped parents in working with and teaching their children at home how to build confidence, how to show humility, how to ward off bullies and how to stop bullying. I have taken well adjusted children and shown them how to excel beyond what they thought was possible. I have helped the extremely timid child step out of their shell and take charge of their life. Children who would never raise their hand to ask a question who now stand up in front of large groups with confidence to speak. I love the potential in all children, and I love the process of being a part of their growth. I love being able to give a parent a few simple tips to help them keep home life fun and to help in any way I can as they work through child rearing. It's something that makes my every day special and fulfilling. I have always said my work is never the same day twice and that is how I like it. Just like kids; fun, energetic, challenging and often unpredictable.

My first experience in teaching Taekwondo was when I was a young (12-year-old), naive assistant to the assistant martial arts instructor in my hometown of Panama City, FL. I had all of two years training in

Taekwondo and my job was to work with the youngest and newest children who came into the studio to learn martial arts. Nervous at first… often my instructor had to correct me, and then I discovered I loved working with people. Those early years is where my passion for teaching and helping others began. I liked learning what motivated the students and how to present my lessons in such a way that made them smile and want to come back for more. Joy for this was so strong that when my father opened his martial arts studio in Fort Walton Beach, I continued my internship as an instructor under his tutelage. I went to every instructor seminar he did and even to this day, I study, train, learn and continue to perfect my chosen craft of instructor and leader. I have studied how to relate to and motivate children of all ages with a varied list of situations, backgrounds and challenges. I have been through 100's of hours of training in working with children outside of martial arts. With all of this and as a child care provider and pre-school teacher in my early years, a church leadership team member for child, teen, and parenting courses… I have seen pretty much all of the issues that kids and parents deal with.

All of this, a lifetime of learning has prepared me for this position and title of Master Mom®. This journey began for me some 40+ years ago and today I spend a good portion of my time training instructors and focusing on helping parents and children not merely survive childhood; but live together as peaceful, cooperative, and loving families.

I see so many parents struggling with disrespectful and disobedient children and I want them to know there is a better way than losing your cool or giving in. Parents will find out here there are steps they can take to cut through the chaos or exhaustion or confusion. Simple things that you can do. Little changes you can make in routine or structure at home that will ease the difficult days. These things you do now will also, more importantly, prevent bigger problems in the future. And whether you are starting when they are infants or teenagers, you can do things to change a negative course, a difficult course into a positive and loving one. That's my goal, my message. To help bring peace and togetherness to families of all types.

I have chosen five topics that I find most families face frequently and causes them a lot of thought and care (and sometimes anxiety): Building Confident Children at Home; Stress in Children and Teens; Quality Family Time; Peer Pressure; Health and Fitness for Kids and Teens. There are a myriad of subtopics under these and if you need help or advice for something not covered or have any questions, please reach out to me at Amanda@AskMasterMom.com, visit my website AskMasterMom.com, or if you are local, check out my academy at OlsonsMA.com. I would love to hear from you, your questions and your success stories of all types. I know we all love to talk about our kids and I am your open door... ready to listen.. ready to advise... and ready for you!

So, from my heart to yours; I wish to help you create a harmonious and happy home.

Sincerely,

Master Mom ® Amanda Olson

Introduction

Thank you reading about *"**Ask Master Mom**"*.

Firstly, I want to say congratulations! You have become the caregiver and role model to a child. This may be as a parent, grandparent, foster parent or other significant person in a child's life.

...Now, what next? What do you really do after that?

You have been given the arduous task of never making a mistake from this moment on and for the rest of your life. Don't feed them the wrong things, don't let them watch the wrong things, make sure they are the smartest, most advanced or most athletic child in everything they do and by all means, make sure they are always perfect little angels whenever any other human being, from the mail man to the school headmaster, is within earshot of you and your children. If you can at least do all of that, you will have mastered parenting!

A little daunting isn't it?

All parents have been embarrassed, appalled and shocked at things their children have done in public. When your child throws up all over your boss, or your eight-year-old blurts out to your best friend, "You smell funny!" Or, your child starts belching loudly at a restaurant, or disrespects you in front of other parents, or sticks her tongue out at the teacher, or tells the pastor that church is boring, or writes about the time you had too much to drink and how funny it was in an essay contest at school and on and on!

See, you are so, not alone! YouTube videos of other people's children are funny until moments like these actually happen to you! Which trust me, they will.

 So how do we handle that? How do we teach them manners, good behavior, common sense without losing our minds?   How do we teach them to be well disciplined, friendly and thoughtful?

That is where I come in, Master Mom, to help save the day and help you become a true master of parenting!

Let's get started!

Building Confident Children at Home

When we think of children with confidence, we think of those children who sing on stage or go on a famous TV talk show and act as if they are in the privacy of their own living room. No inhibitions, no fear; just boldness and self-assurance. Those are pretty high standards and not really the norm.

I remember as a kid hoping at one of those come up on stage dinner theater shows to never get called up on stage from the audience. It was a huge fear of mine and I would slink down in my chair hoping no one would see me. It worked!

However, that fear carried over into the classroom and I was afraid to raise my hand and ask a question. Or worse, have the teacher call on me for an answer. Not that I didn't know the answer, but I knew my face would turn red, I would start sweating and a frog the size of my fist would lodge in my throat. It's an awful way to go through school.

I also remember a pivotal moment in high-school when I decided I was tired of being afraid. I decided to just start raising my hand, asking questions and putting that "pick me, pick me" look on my face that every teacher hopes to see from their students. It was just a switch. I decided to stop caring what others thought. I literally made the decision to stop being afraid. It worked. My body can still have those physical tell-tale signs of nerves like blushing or sweeting, but the frog never really showed up and I took on the "fake it 'till you make it" mentality. Interestingly enough, public speaking is one of my strengths as an adult.

As a teacher I can really identify with the child in the group who is shy. That's the child I call upon. The quiet ones who know all the answers. I also encourage the ones who shut down and refuse to speak or move. It takes time. A gradual culling of the nerves, extra support and praise but most times, it results in the child being able to stand up and speak or perform. I know the freedom that confidence gives, and I know the bondage the lack of it can bring. That's why it is such an important topic for me. I've learned to live in freedom of fear and want to help others do the same.

Be Honest And Straightforward

Children accept what is around them and make it their own. If you endeavor to be smiley, pleasant and friendly to others your child will get the idea. Teach eye contact by doing it. Be honest and straightforward, make the rules clear before you start anything and have lots of fun times. Expect people to be friendly and they almost always will be. Point out the good bits of disappointing situations and your children will do likewise, for example, "The match was cancelled because of the weather, now we have more time to make our Christmas cards."

Make Them Feel Secured

Your child needs to feel secure. This is achieved by being there for your kids, listening to them, giving them quality time, making it clear that you think they are great and showing how much you enjoy them and value their company. When your children want some attention, give it to them wholeheartedly. Look at them and give them your full attention. Children are more responsive to voice tone and attitude than to what you actually say! So don't waste words when a smile and a hand hold is all that is needed. If there is some distraction - cooking on the stove, baby crying, somewhere to get to in a hurry, then promise attention at a specific time later and keep your promise.

Try To Always Listen To Them

Being able to listen to children is a brilliant skill to have. If a child says something like, "I'm no good at math" then don't contradict this by saying "Oh I think you do very well in math" as this ends the conversation and the child gets no chance to explore with you what is actually going on. A better response is "Oh dear - you are feeling bad about the math today." Then, with any luck, your child will elaborate on how he or she feels and you are in a position to offer support.

Help Them Overcome Fear

So, for parents of shy children, let's talk about how to help them overcome that fear. We talk about "building" confidence and this is very true. Building your confidence takes practice but the really cool thing is, is that every time you practice, even a little, you build more confidence. The only thing you really need is a tiny bit of guts and faith to take one small step forward. Then you can push yourself into a world of freedom to pursue the life you want and really deserve.

Support Is Also Very Crucial

Knowing that someone will be there after you launch yourself into the world to help you recover is so very important. For the child who is afraid, helping them learn to try is essential. Not pushing them or forcing them, but patiently supporting them. Sometimes that may mean you need to do something new with them. Volunteer to coach or work in the classroom. Go on the field trips or sit in the audience. I did a lot of performing in school and knowing I had friends and/or family in the audience really boosted my confidence. I knew at least one person out there would think I was amazing!

Give Your Children Feedback

Feedback is also key in helping to build confidence. Let your child know how proud you are of them when they take a chance. Let them talk about the experience and reward their efforts. As I mentioned before, you can build your confidence with practice, just like anything else. Start small, take little steps and then build up slowly. Also, talk about the failures. I remember one time when I was singing, and my voice cracked. Someone came up to me afterwards and said, that was great except for that one note. So, my failure was noticed but I lived to tell about it! Seriously though, I would not recommend that type of feedback. I once heard a make-up artist say, stop looking at the magnifying mirror to get ready in the morning, no one can see all of those flaws and it just makes you feel ugly! Truth! The same relates to feedback to your kids. Focus on the positive and let a lot of those little insignificant things go that no one really pays attention to anyway.

Encourage Them To Feel Good About Themselves And Their Achievements

Building confidence is about encouraging children to feel good about themselves and their achievements. Avoid putting children in positions of failure. Create tasks that can be achieved and make them achievable by giving appropriate support. If the game is to hit a ball with a bat then find a bat that is so big and a ball that is so soft that success is inevitable. Once the child can do this, make it more difficult - perhaps hitting the ball past a tree or using a slightly smaller bat. If the task is to encourage reading then the same rule applies - make sure your child can achieve success somehow. Make the book appropriate and achievable. Don't let your child struggle - read a page each or read alongside your child, help them to succeed. Confidence will come as one small success builds on another. Praise is no use unless the child feels he or she has earned it. Create situations to make success happen.

The achievable tasks you present to your children need not be of the academic or sporting variety. Perhaps looking after a pet or younger sibling may be more appropriate, or playing in a co-operative way, or making something, or helping with a household job like cooking or washing the car.

Use realistice and specific praise, really mean it. Say, "I like the way you've chopped those carrots" rather that blanket praise like, "That's nice dear." Pick out something specific on which to comment favourably. Always do that first. If there is room for improvement set another challenge - eg "Next time you can do the onions too" (or whatever). Children need to know they are doing OK but at the same time they like to feel they are moving towards a higher goal and that you trust they will get there! I use this technique multiple times a day in my martial arts classes and teach instructors to do the same. Giving specific praise for a job well done really does make a world of difference than a blanket "good job".

Being able to approach a variety of situations with confidence makes life so much more pleasant, relaxed and interesting whatever the situation - at work, social events, learning something new or having time with family and friends. The skills needed to feel confident, self-reliant and assured can be taught to children from a young age and will stand them in good stead for a whole lifetime. Teaching these skills to your children is straightforward, fun and rewarding and will give them skills to build upon as they grow and mature.

Stress in Children And Teens

Everyone has stressful days. Days where nothing seems to go right, you're running behind, the refrigerator breaks, the kids are going crazy and you have an important deadline to meet. All you want is a quiet place to sit and do nothing, to calm down and feel the cool breeze on your stressed-out tired face. This, however, is not the type of stress I would like to address in this chapter. The stress I am talking about is the type that affects your health and affects your ability to function comfortably at home, school, work, or social situations. The type of chronic stress that brings tears or outburst on a daily basis. That type, the type of stress that stops you from participating in the things you normally do or would like to participate in. This of course can lead to depression which can be very difficult to overcome.

Each Child is Different

Everyone is wired differently, and our children are no exception. Everything that causes you stress can also cause them stress. On the other hand, they are individuals and understanding what causes them to become stressed is important to understand. A simple example; being late to anything causes my daughter a lot of stress. The stress manifest itself by putting her in an agitative state. My son, however, tends to be completely unaffected in the same situation. I bring this up because it is very important to understand the differences in your children, even how they are different from you. Because I know this about my daughter and she knows it, we can work towards doing what we can to make sure we are on time. As a grown woman now, she knows this about herself and takes steps on her own to be on time and gets a lot of stress relief by planning ahead.

Stress Can Hinder Performance

If your child is in a stressful state, it makes it extremely difficult to perform at school or other activities to the best of their abilities. Imagine having to give a speech after your best friend just dumped all of their problems on you, making you late so you didn't have time to organize your thoughts before being thrust on stage with expectations to be brilliant. A nightmare, right? When kids arrive at school after having a stressful morning, it is very difficult for them to focus their best and they will have difficulty socializing. We just need to understand as parents, how our kids function and how we can help them be their very best.

Talk About It / Take a Time-Out

There is a lot of pressure on children of all ages to behave well, make good grades, perform well at their chosen extra-curricular activities, apply themselves and make good friends; along with a myriad of other things. If your child or teen is showing signs of stress, it is time to stop, talk about it and make an action plan to fix it. It may mean that you need to cut back on something to relieve time management stress or it may mean making a schedule and a game plan for each day. You may also find that some intervention with a classmate, teacher or even some counseling is in order. Whatever the answer is, taking a time-out to discover the cause and find a solution is very important for the health, growth and happiness of your child. You have to think of chronic stress the same way you would think of an illness. You wouldn't let pneumonia go unchecked or untreated. Don't allow stress to do long term damage to your child and family either. It's just as deadly with long-term consequences.

One Family's Example

I worked with a family and their 5-year-old some years back. The boy was having trouble relaxing at night to go to bed and through talking we discovered that he was insecure about what the next day would bring. He didn't know if it was a school day or not and if he was going to his sports practice or if the babysitter was coming, things like that. We devised a calendar to put on his bedroom door with pictures of what was happening each day so he could know in advance what was going to happen. Because he couldn't read yet, on school days there was a picture of a schoolhouse. They put a picture of a church on Sunday, a picture of a karate guy for martial arts days, and a smiley face for Saturdays. It seems simple but it really helped the little boy and enjoyed looking at and making his calendar each month. He eventually grew out of the need for the pictures and understood the concept of days of the week and weekend, but for that time in his life, it was important to address his stress.

Build Trust

Now granted, at that level, stress is not life-threatening. However, the mother learned what was causing the stress and knew what to look for in the future. The boy learned that his mom cared about his well-being and was there to help him. This is a small action with a powerful result of building trust and understanding between parent and child.

Relationship Stress

Another area that can be the cause of stress is that of relationships. Learning how to get along with others, knowing who safe people are to hang out with, and finding a peer group you can connect with is not easy for a lot of children. Younger children are very self-centered individuals and they are learning that they can't always get their way. If they are slow to learn this, other children will not want to play with them or be their friend because they will look at them as being mean and not nice. It's important for you to teach them to care about others. Being disliked by others can cause a lot of stress. Take time to observe how your child interacts with others on the playground or on the team. How kind and cooperative are they? Are they letting others push them around? Stay in touch with how they are doing at school and how well they are getting along with others in their class. It may be something simple like a conversation on how to behave or something much more complicated like needing to change classes because of a bully.

Belonging to a Group

As for teenagers and young adults, fitting in and belonging to a peer group is so very important to them. This is a time when kids really learn who they are becoming, how the world perceives them and how to handle conflicts. I have a unique position as a martial arts instructor to works with lots of teenagers. I enjoy this age group because they are full of potential and ideas and wonder. Helping them learn how to communicate, how to be themselves and how to accept others is a rewarding thing to be a part of. In my decades of work with teenagers there is one aspect of their age group that has never changed. They want to be accepted for who they are, even as they are really just figuring that out for themselves. Culturally, terms like jock, nerd, airhead and preppy came into being in the 50's and 60's in the U.S. Movies and books portray teens as being labeled into a certain group in high school and each is associated with a specific stereotype. The need to belong and identify with a certain group is a powerful influence on children at this age have to deal with.

Actively Seek Positive Peer Groups

My advice would be to actively seek peer groups you believe would be a positive influence on your teen. I know many of my martial arts students who come to me as teenagers are coming for that very reason. Their parents want them to find positive role models and be in an environment that encourages respect for others as well as themselves. A place where they can learn a really cool art that will empower them and also protect them from bullying or other dangers. I know the teens in my martial arts classes always arrive early to talk and "hang out". I love seeing them make friends, become comfortable socially and feel comfortable around peers and adults. I can speak from years of experience when I say a quality, character focused martial arts program can benefit a teen in ways no other program can. They learn self-discipline, kindness, cooperativeness and confidence to last a lifetime.

If you are a parent of a teenager, then you must know that teens today are facing far more pressure than teens years ago. Their demand for time has become increasingly greater and the pressure to succeed and to get ahead of their peers is enormous. When you factor in the stresses of simply being a teenager who is trying to find your place in society, it is no wonder that teens today constantly feel overwhelmed and tired out by their work. Giving your children and loved ones advice on how to manage teenage stress effectively is important, as most are never willing to ask for help and suffer negative consequences as a result.

Provide A Stress Relief Outlet

One of the first things that you should do for your teen is to give them an outlet to relief their stress. Your teenager is constantly bombarded with text messages, cell phone calls, emails, IM's, and My space requests, just to name a few. Everyone needs time to recharge and this is especially true for your stressed out teen. You should get him or her interested in another form of activity that completely enables one to be away from their otherwise more stressful demands or work. Such activities can range from reading a book, participating in a sport, to any other extracurricular activity such as choir or perhaps the band.

If you are unable to find an activity which your teen finds interesting, then you should consider making it mandatory that all work and stress come to a pause for at least one hour each evening at home. Your children may complain that they do not have the time to stop working; however, giving them the time and the space to relax is very important. It is definitely an effective way of helping them manage teenage stress.

Always Be There To Assist Your Children

Another thing you can do is to ensure that your teen knows that you are always there for him or her. Keeping all lines of communication open, between you and your child is extremely important. Remember to listen carefully and let them vent whatever frustrations they have when they do come to you. This is because, research shows that one of the biggest complaints from teens is that their parents either minimize their problems or do not make any effort to understand what they are saying or where they are coming from.

Help Them Find A Trusted Guidance Counselor

Also, let your child know that if he or she feels uncomfortable talking to you about certain things or events that have impacted their lives, then he or she should seek advice from another trusted adult. You could always suggest a guidance counselor at school, a youth pastor at church, or perhaps a favorite Aunt or Uncle. This gives them the sense that they can always get help through other means even though they do not wish to tell you what the exact problem is. This will be effective in managing their stress as they will not end up bottling too many emotions or think that they are suffering alone in the situation.

Be Conscious About Ill Health & Fitness issues

If you are in anxiety making situations you might experience a brief compromise to your stress threshold that needs management. You may observe an issue with your health and symptoms may range from slight anxiety to more worrying medical concerns which could require professional advice. Most health care professionals suggest keeping a stress journal to enable you to chart your stress threshold and find out what your stressors are. Stressors are the situations which cause your stress threshold to decrease, you generally respond to them or you are triggered by them. One course of action is to avoid unnecessary stress and deal with difficulties with additional coping mechanisms. Your younger child may not be able to keep a stress journal but you can keep one for them.

Help your child by getting them involved in physical activity. By increasing your fitness levels not only can you ensure your physical body is able to handle the stresses and strains of modern life; your emotional well being will probably be increased too. The benefits of working out are that it reduces many of the harmful chemicals in your body which are triggered by stressful situations. Research shows how the more sedentary we get the less our bodies and minds are able to cope with stress, and this could be responsible for anxiety and depression. Going for a run, gentle exercise etc. are all known to reduce levels of stress and increase well being. The consequence of aerobic activity is the best known way of relaxing because of the inhaling of air; however these really should not be overdone or put undue stress on other regions of your body. Keep in mind, if you begin a new exercise routine make sure you have had a complete physical in advance.

Seek Healthy Recipes & Nutrition

In addition to raising your consumption of good and nutritious food many people often seek out recipes that are easy and quick with stress busting ingredients, good for the entire family. Pay particular attention to stress related allergies and make sure that you can allow time to incorporate family eating together time. This is important for those who have growing children; especially as children who will be developing need to eat well, as good food can heavily influence the growth, behaviour, health and well being of growing children. Young children and teens experiencing growth spurts really should have food that is based upon essential food sources. Quick starts to this are by reducing caffeine and sugar, increasing foods which are said to lower cholesterol which fattens the arteries and makes heighten adrenaline levels more dangers and consuming more calming spices and herbs such as cinnamon, cocoa and leafy green vegetables. Picky eaters can be catered for by using online recipe finders and trying different recipes, including children's help in making family meals will assist with this and education them nutritionally and into independence, lessening stress on care givers that do the majority of the cooking in the long run.

Make Time For Fun

How you think really does matter and tests have shown that men and women who have a positive outlook on life tend to suffer less from the effects of stress. Indulging in good humour regularly is also said to make a difference to your feelings. The "lighten up" effect of having fun has been proven in tests and research to have a positive effect on lowering anxiety and lessening the likelihood of low feelings. Don't stop playing games together with your children when they reach a certain age, it can be more essential than ever before to learn new technology with them and experience a selection of their video games and music as they grow into adulthood and even reading together and doing fun family things to strengthen the bonds of child and parent/ care giver should never stop.

Know How to Help

Teenagers today face an immense amount stress in their daily lives. There is constant pressure to do well in school, get accepted into college, get scholarships to pay for it, keep a part time job as well as keep a social life. Many teens cannot handle stress on their own, so parents who know how to manage teenage stress effectively will help to eliminate some of the problems that they are facing. As I have said before, stay in touch with your child's life, talk about their day, how they are doing, and who their friends are. This type of caring communication can go a long way in warding off harmful long-term stress.

Create Quality Family Time

When I think back on my childhood in elementary school, I have fond memories of spending some great time with my parents and younger brother. We went camping and boating, played ball in the front yard, hung out at the beach and went to the movies. We played board games and card games, traveled and genuinely enjoyed being together. Not to say it was all roses and butterflies. My brother and I had to be assigned my side and his side in the back seat on car trips, got in trouble arguing about silly stuff and even got grounded a few times. There were times when my dad got us lost or mom lost her cool. Times when parks were closed, or we just missed the last ferry to Disney. But those are the times, along with the best of them, that we all can look back on and laugh about.

I grew up your typical latch-key kid in the 70's and 80's and spent a lot of time doing things after school like girl scouts and soccer. In the summer I went to various relatives for a week, enjoyed summer camps and hanging out at home playing baseball in the front yard and riding my bike. Both of my parent's worked fulltime jobs and even some part-time jobs to make extra money. My mom was going to college at night and spent a lot of time on the weekends studying and doing homework.

So, in short, it wasn't like I spent all of my non-school time with my family. I am mentioning this because despite our family's busy lives, my parents made it a priority to make the time we did have count. As a family we cleaned the house, worked in the yard, went to church, and made the most of our free time by having fun. We learned to work together, play together and live together as a happy unit. To this day I enjoy getting together with my family and now that my brother and I have children of our own, it just keeps getting more and more fun.

Planning Ahead

In order to create the freedom to have more time available to dedicate to family time, you often need a little pre-planning. Have a "fun" money fund for unexpected opportunities that pop up so you can take that family outing or quick weekend getaway without straining your budget. I remember a time when my parents surprised my brother and I with a night at the amusement park. We had been there before but this one stuck out as extra fun because it was unexpedted. I don't know if my parents got some extra time off or received a bonus, but they used that moment to create a great family memory.

Another planning tip is to involve the kids. When my children were young, we planned a trip to Disney. They knew weeks in advance about and we got out the maps and information together around the kitchen table. We talked about rides or shows we wanted to be sure to see. Each of my children had a special piggy bank to save up money for souvenirs. They did little chores around the house to earn money and of course grandparents chipped in. When it came time for the trip, everyone was excited because they knew they would experience something they had been thinking about and planning for weeks. The kids were also excited about having money to spend on items of their own choosing. It was a great family teamwork time and we had lots of fun in the planning and adventure.

Learn to Delegate

Freeing up some time for yourself as a parent can really help everyone. You are in a better mood and have the energy to do the extra fun things with the kids. It's hard to have the energy to play catch or ride bikes when you've been cleaning, doing yardwork or laundry all day. Assign a few chores to everyone, and you might be amazed how much more free time you have. Of course, teaching everyone the skills they will need to perform the chores might take a bit more time in the beginning. But, once everyone gets in the swing of things, you'll probably wish you had taught everyone how to help out a lot sooner. Try to include even the youngest family members, to avoid leaving anyone out. Although they might only be able to perform the simplest of chores, it's important that they be made to feel like they are part of the family "team." You could even display the chores lists in picture frames on the wall, so that everyone can see how they can help.

Maintain a Family Calendar

Keeping a family calendar that everyone can refer to can be a great way to save time. If you've ever made three separate car trips when one could have sufficed, you probably have a good idea of how poor planning can waste time. Create a family calendar and schedule, place in picture frames, and display prominently on the wall. That way, everyone can see what everyone else is doing in a single glance. Hanging a large envelope beside the calendar as a handy spot to keep tickets, schedules, maps, and other items that are relevant to everybody's schedules is also a good idea. I know some larger families who have a big bulletin board for the families monthly schedule of activites.

Treat Yourself to Some Leisure Time

Once you've implemented a few time saving tips, celebrate your newly discovered free time by planning a fun leisure time activity for the entire family. Plan a short family vacation, go on a picnic, or just take a walk through the neighborhood park. Be sure to take a few photos of your family enjoying these activities together.

Then, display them in picture frames throughout your home, as a reminder of the effectiveness of your new time saving methods. Once everyone realizes how much fun these free time activities can be, they will probably be even more enthusiastic about implementing additional time saving methods.

Participate In Outdoor Activities

There are so many things that a family can do to unite. For instance, you can start to participate in outdoor activities that all of you are fond of. Outdoor fun includes swimming, theme parks, bird watching, water sports, hiking, camping, and so much more. These activitys of course lead to stress release as an added bonus!

Engage In Do-It-Yourself Projects

You can also consider undertaking various exciting do-it-yourself projects, such as building models, making photo collages, painting ceramics, or starting a good home improvement project. Rich and fulfilling family events are something that is never forgotten. Just remember to take lot's of pictures (or even videos) of your fun activity, so that you can also enjoy looking through them together in the future.

Another all-time favorite are board games. There are dozens of great board games for the entire family to play together. Younger players could enjoy the popular Thomas and Friends DVD Bingo while older players could refresh their grip on good old Monopoly. You can even go online and look for do it yourself escape rooms at home and even mystery "who done it" games where everyone gets to play a character. So many options for unique family time games.

Working Parent Guilt

There is a lot of information out there that can make you feel guilty for working outside the home or that you should have X number of hours of dinner time each week. Well, as a latch key kid with two working parents and lots of great memories, it's all about the quality, not the quantity. You can relax. Make the time you do get together count. If you do stay home, mom or dad, the same is true. Sometimes it is not the parents who are busy but the kids! Make the time you have count by doing things together whether it's a big vacation or stay in movie, pizza night. I never once thought that my parents didn't spend enough time with me as a kid. We were all just living as a family doing the best each could do.

On another note, if you don't have what may be considered a traditional family, make a family of your own with friends and other relatives. I know many people who find themselves transplanted into communities where they know no one. They make friends, get involved with groups and organizations and create a network of support and friendships outside of the bloodline, if you will. Family is a feeling. That's what you want to create, an atmosphere of family, of bonding and trust between people. You can do that. You can give your children the comforting sense of family.

Strong family bonding is essential for each of its members. Families that don't spend much time together are missing out on a lot of things. Try to talk more, keep your communication channel open, share your thoughts and dreams, keep up to date on each other's lives, and spend quality family time together.

Peer Pressure

"But everyone else was doing it!" An extremely frustrating phrase for parents to hear. You think your rules, your values, your lines in the sand are well known to your kids. Well, in my mind they are well known, this particular phrase is one that children use to justify their actions and think you will agree with them that if everyone else is doing it, it must be okay. Just like everything, kids must be taught. They learn a lot through observing, through learning what is and is not allowed or acceptable. But they must have a serious sit-down conversation of rules and laws of the land spoken in plain English (or the language of your choice), often and with eye contact. I like to have my kids repeat back to me what I just said so I know for a fact they got it. That way, there can be no further excuses for "doing what everyone else does."

Fitting In

There are many reasons why kids fall prey to peer pressure. The most obvious is to fit in and be accepted. This happens to all of us. We've laughed at an off-color joke, gossiped, any number of things. We are all guilty. It gets dangerous however when kids from a very early age don't build confidence in themselves and have a sense of being okay without having to fit in. They can easily fall into substance abuse, thrill seeking dangers like speeding or shoplifting, or sex. We all know how dangerous these things can be for our teens and the time to start preparing them for NOT giving in to peer pressure is when they are young. Talk about it with your six-year-old. Let them know they have a safe place to land (you) if they get laughed at or left out because they didn't want to follow along.

Stay in Touch

If you are dealing with a teen or older child, stay on top of things. Help them find good friends and good places to hang out. Teens and pre-teens want to be in groups and if they are not accepted, they will find a group who will accept them. And, unlike when I was a child, they can find these groups online and on social media. Just as dangerous as any face to face encounter can be. Make your home a place where kids can come and hang out while you are there. Make sure if they are hanging out with friends you know who these kids are. What are they in to? Ask questions. It's not spying, it is protecting; and as a parent on the other side of this, trust me; they will be grateful for your protection later.

Fear of Being Bullied

Another reason children fall for peer pressure is because of fear. They are afraid if they don't "join in" they may be hurt. Maybe someone is bullying, and they join in so they aren't the one being bullied. Or, someone stronger or with more power is forcing them to do something they don't want to do and feel powerless to stop. In these situations, some real intervention from a counselor, school official or other trusted authority figure may be needed. If someone, such as your teen, lacks in confidence or support, it can be very easy for them to fall in with the wrong crowd. Teens especially need confidence and support to feel and be secure with who they are and the choices they are making.

As a parent, you are your child's immediate and most important support system, and can help them stay grounded. While it is important for your child to be social, you must also teach them to know when and how to draw the line. Here are some things you can do to help your child be better prepared to deal with peer pressur:

Set A Good Example Ourselves

Children learn more from what we do than what we say. If we're always busy trying to keep up with the Joneses, we can't expect our children to say no to pressure from their own peers. If we keep buying the latest designer brands simply because fashion magazines tell us to, we can't teach our children to resist the peer pressure of spending beyond their means. We have to stand our ground before we can instill the will and the power in our children to resist peer pressure.

Help Children Select The Right Role Models In Mass Media

Engage in meaningful discussions with your children after you read a book, watch TV, see a movie, or pass a billboard together. Talk to them about what they like or dislike about the characters in stories, shows, or ads. Explore with them whom they want to be like when they grow up and why. To help you get started, the Enchanted Collar books come with a full set of worksheets to help parents guide their children through the moral lessons embedded in the stories.

Provide Unwavering Emotional Support To Your Children

They must have an internal moral compass to steer clear of treacherous paths. They need a solid foundation, an emotional "rock," someone confident enough to withstand peer pressure. Be that rock for your children. On your car/subway/train trips together, ask them about the events of their day at school. Talk to them about what they did, how they felt, and how they could have reacted differently if necessary. Listen to them with an open heart. Look at things through their eyes. Walk a mile in their shoes. Above all, keep reminding them that when the crowd goes mad, they don't have to give in to peer pressure and go mad too.

Communicate Often

A non-judgemental conversation with your child about their choices and friends will help you better understand their situation. Don't be too harsh with critiquing your child, even if you happen to notice any sudden, unfavourable changes in their behaviour; criticism will only shut your child out, making it harder for you to understand them. Instead, be firm and compassionate in trying to understand what your child is really going through, so you can talk them through the process.

Build Up Their Self-Esteem

A child with a strong sense of self will be less likely to be led astray by their peer group. Teenagers often feel pressured to join with their peers in doing something wrong because they don't feel like they belong. A clique - even if it's doing bad things can give teens with a low self esteem an important part of acceptance. Being part of a group helps your teen fell like he belongs to something.

Know Who Your Child's Friends Are

Don't relegate your knowledge of your child's peer group to faceless names. Invite your child's friends over occasionally, and take the time to learn about their families. If possible, initiate conversations with the parents of your child's friends so that you have a clearer idea of their backgrounds and values, and know to watch for potential red flags.

Encourage Your Child To Participate In Hobbies And Activities That They Like

The possibility of your child meeting like-minded friends increases exponentially in such scenarios. Here, your child will find it easier to be themselves, instead of squeezing their personalities into a mould, to be able to fit in.

Teach your child the importance of saying 'No'

Your child should know that it is okay to distance themselves from any activity or person that they aren't comfortable with. Also talk about the consequences of saying 'No' to your child: too many children buckle under the pressure of being excluded from the 'cool group'. Let your child know that you will always be there to love and support them unconditionally, even when it feels like the entire world is going the other way. Finally, talk your child through various uncomfortable scenarios that they might encounter, and demonstrate to them how and when they can decline from participating.

Set Clear Boundaries

At the end of the day, your child will model their behaviour on the example that you set for them. Set clear boundaries about what is and isn't considered acceptable in your household. Your child must be aware of these boundaries and be taught to respect them. Be strict and firm with any deviations, so that your child is clear about your expectations from him/her.

Don't be afraid to mediate

Many parents are reluctant to interfere with their children's social group, for fear that it will alienate their child even further. However, should the need arise, don't hesitate to involve yourself in the situation. Talk to the other children's parents or your child's school teachers about any problematic behaviours that you think are stemming from your child's peer group. If necessary, limit the amount of time your child is allowed to spend with children you consider a negative influence.

Encourage your child's positive choices

Children thrive on encouragement and positive reinforcement. Let your child know when they are making good choices, so that they instinctively gravitate towards similar actions and people.

Teach your child the importance of compassion

A child who is sympathetic to their peers will also be quicker to recognize situations where they are being treated unfairly. Teaching your child about compassion will also prevent them from indulging in behaviours that could be detrimental to the wellbeing of others.

Peer pressure is not just applicable to adolescents and teens, but can also affect much younger children. In toddlers and pre-schoolers for instance, peer pressure may demonstrate itself by way of social exclusion, which your child may either suffer or be a part of. If unattended, this can negatively impact your child's self-confidence and make them more gullible in their later years. Begin talking to your child about peer pressure early, and keep these channels of communication open so that your child has all the tools he/she needs to become a confident, well-adjusted human being.

Health And Fitness For Kids And Teens

It's true that many children this age have a lot of homework - nevertheless, it's important to be active. Like adult fitness, teen fitness is important for physical and mental health. But as kids grow up the level of physical activity tends to decline. For teenagers to be healthy they need to perform at least 60 minutes of moderate exercise a day. However, keeping fit and healthy is not always a priority for teenagers coping with the pressures of adolescence. Here are some tips for fitness for your pre-teen and why it's so important.

Exercise Is No Longer a Built-In Part of the Day

Today's middle-aged adults may find themselves fighting a stubborn middle-age spread. Former high school track stars have evolved into busy parents who juggle careers and families and it's hard to keep up the fitness levels we once had. But when we were young, many of us were more active. We rode bikes to our friends' houses and spent hours running around and playing outside. If we wanted to watch a movie, we had to actually get up and go to a theater or make a trip to the video rental store. If we wanted to play video games, many of us went to an arcade often traveling by bike to get there.

Compare that to today's kids, who have everything they need for hours of entertainment conveniently located in their family computer or smartphone. Even buying things can be done with the click of a mouse. As a result, today's kids are inherently more sedentary than past generations. The exercise we got naturally through bike rides to our friends' houses and playing outside are not a necessary part of their daily life. Exercise has to be planned, fitted in. It's an additional activity, not a natural part of the process.

Set Up Healthy Habits

Establishing fitness habits at an early age can lay the foundation for a lifetime of healthy habits. A pre-teen is still malleable. The habits you instill now as a parent are habits that will continue with your child for a lifetime. If you teach your children the importance of being active and your child and your family lead an active lifestyle, your children will simply get in the habit of running, exercising, and keeping fit. And this habit will be likely to continue through college and adulthood.

Fitness Is Psychologically Important

Pre-teens are in the awkward years. Exercise can boost confidence, release endorphins, reduce that antsy pent-up energy kids this age get, alleviate tension, and boost confidence. The teenage years are a great time to introduce the importance of regular exercise. Patterns of behaviour that begin during adolescence are likely to continue through to adult life. Young people should be encouraged to enjoy physical activities that offer variety and enjoyment and are suitable for their age.

It is found that inactive teenagers have higher levels of body fat, lower levels of fitness and are more likely to suffer depression. Schools are assigning less time for teens to participate in sport so exercise alternatives need to be found outside of education.

Going to the gym will help teenagers to maintain fitness. Several gym membership packages include entrance to swimming pools and exercise classes offering a wide variety of physical activity. Yet some 13-19 year olds will find it difficult to commit to a structured gym environment and membership may be expensive.

Team sports are great for kids this age to achieve the recommended levels of physical exercise. For those not interested in being on a team, there are many individual sports they can choose from. One that comes to mind right away for me is martial arts! I have lots of students who love the fact that they are participating 100% of the time in the class. No waiting around or sitting on the bench. Golf and tennis are also great options for sports that don't necessarily require a team.

Whether the confidence comes from knowing your child can outrun a bully or whether from knowing he or she is healthy, strong and fit, fitness is a definite bonus. Who wouldn't want to equip their child with extra confidence as you send them to middle school?

Improve Grades

Studies have shown that children who are active in their pre-teen years from age eleven on average do better on some academic tests. They also found that these kids continue to do well on tests several years later because they exercised when they were eleven. I believe that the focus required to do a physical skill like hitting a ball, paying attention to rules and mentally preparing for a challenge is one reason that academics can improve because of sports.

There are many reasons establishing a habit of fitness for your pre-teen. Not only will your child gain a foundation of healthy living if you establish fitness habits at an early age, but she will also benefit from cardiovascular health, improved grades, a surge in confidence and psychological well-being.

Whether you encourage your child to take part in a school sport, an independent activity such as golf or martial arts or simply encourage her to ride her bike, run or help with yard care, encouraging your child to be active will make a big difference in her life.

Enagage Them In Regular Recreational And Competitive Team Activities

Most schools offer regular recreational and competitive team activities. By introducing competition into exercise, teens will be motivated to work harder and be the best in the team.

Teens should be encouraged to play a variety of sports that can be played all year round. Team games are fun and teenagers enjoy exercising with friends. Group sports can be continued out of education so look out for local recreational teams and leagues.

Not everyone is interested in competitive sport so introduce teens to different activities such as karate, dance or skateboarding as kids at this age like to try new things. Even if a hobby isn't physically demanding it will help to maintain fitness.

Physical activity must be matched with healthy eating and for adolescents a balanced diet is imperative. Adolescence is a time of rapid growth and the major dietary requirement is for energy rich food. The body needs to get the right amount of nutrients through a balance of starch, dairy, fruit, vegetables and proteins.

During puberty teenagers body concerns are intensified and studies have reported that teenagers are more likely to become unhappy with their weight.

Maintaining levels of nutrition are important and if kids need to lose weight then cutting down on fat and sugar based foods is a way to do so.

Regular physical activity increases the likelihood of teenagers remaining healthy in adulthood. They should find ways to be active everyday as the onset of chronic diseases like diabetes can begin to develop early in life. Teens can keep active by going to the gym or playing team sports. Simply walking to school will promote fitness.

Conclusion

"What did one Rocket Scientist say to the other Rocket Scientist?"

"Relax, it's not Parenting!"

Raising children is the most important job in the world and raising children is a wonderful and challenging life experience. It is also one of those jobs you don't understand until you have children of your own. I know for myself; I now understand why my mom always said, "Be Safe.", every time I left the house. I thought she was overprotective. Today, I still say this to my kids even though they are approaching 30!

I tell parents all the time: As you go through this journey with your children, you will at first be all knowing in their eyes. Keeper of all of life's answers. Then, as they grow into teenagers, all of a sudden you are the least intelligent, and most out of touch human on earth. And finally, when they go to buy their first home or car or have kids of their own; it comes full circle and you again, have so much knowledge. It's a cycle that I've lived through with my own children and have seen it happen so many times in my students. I remember a parent telling me about helping their child apply for college. She said, "Seems like you need a college degree just to fill out the paperwork!" Our children will need us well beyond high school so establishing a strong sense of family will continue to be important.

As parents, we play a very important role in raising children in a safe and loving environement. When parents recognize and deal with their children's most challenging traits in a positive manner, they go a long way in building up a child to be confident and happy. All parents face challenges in raising children. There is no exception. Don't be afraid to connect with others for support, it's always good to have a knowledgeable friend or mentor.

Creating a stable family environment and raising children should be a joy. The family of a child, however you define it, is critical for development in all stages of life. My hope for each family, and the reason I write about family, is so that you will, no matter the challenges, ultimately have a harmonious and happy home.

Yours Truly,

Amanda Olson — Master Mom®

Made in the USA
Coppell, TX
25 November 2019